# The Mask of Anarchy

## Five Leaves Bookshop Occasional Papers

**The Current Status of Jerusalem** by Edward Said
978-1-910170-09-0, 32 pages, £4

**Doctor Who and the Communist: Malcolm Hulke and his career in television** by Michael Herbert
978-1-910170-08-3, 32 pages, £4

**Strengthening Democracy in Post-conflict Northern Ireland** by Maria Power
978-1-910170-16-8, 32 pages, £4

**Anarchy 38: Nottingham** by Freedom Press
978-1-910170-18-2, 32 pages, £4

**How We Live and How We Might Live** by William Morris
978-1-910170-26-7, 28 pages, £4

**Harper Lee and the American South** by Katie Hamilton
978-1-910170-27-4, 28 pages, £4

**That Precious Strand of Jewishness that Challenges Authority** by Leon Rosselson
978-1-910170-33-5, 28 pages, £4

**Mad John's Walk** by John Gallas
978-1-910170-41-0, 16 pages, £3

**Street Haunting** by Virginia Woolf & **Bulwell** by Stanley Middleton
978-1-910170-42-7, 24 pages, £4

**The Mask of Anarchy** by Percy Bysshe Shelley
978-1-910170-48-9, 28 pages, £4

**The Fear of Being Seen as White Losers** by David Jackson
978-1-910170-54-0, 42 pages, £6

**Byron Speaks up for the Luddites** by Lord Byron
978-1-910170-59-5, 24 pages, £4

Available from Five Leaves or from other bookshops worldwide.
All prices include UK postage if ordered direct from
Five Leaves Bookshop.

www.fiveleavesbookshop.co.uk

# The Mask of Anarchy

*Percy Bysshe Shelley*
with an introduction by John Lucas

Five Leaves Bookshop Occasional Papers

**The Mask of Anarchy**
*by Percy Bysshe Shelley*

Written in 1819, first published in 1832
This edition published in 2017
and reprinted in 2019+
by Five Leaves Bookshop
14a Long Row, Nottingham NG1 2DH
www.fiveleavesbookshop.co.uk

Five Leaves Bookshop Occasional Paper 10
ISBN: 978-1-910170-48-9

Introduction copyright © John Lucas, 2017

Designed and typeset by Five Leaves Bookshop

Printed in Great Britain

# The Mask of Anarchy – Introduction
## *John Lucas*

> I met Murder on the way
> He had a mask like Castlereagh—
> Very smooth he looked, yet grim;
> Seven blood-hounds followed him:
>
> All were fat; and well they might
> Be in admirable plight,
> For one by one, and two by two,
> He tossed them human hearts to chew
> Which from his wide cloak he drew.

There is a case to be made for Robert Stewart Castlereagh (1769–1821), Viscount of Londonderry, diplomatist, sometime Keeper of the Privy Seal, MP for County Down, and Tory big-wig. Recent historians in particular have been kinder to him than used to be the case. It was, they remind us, Castlereagh who, as the English representative of Lord Liverpool's Administration, became the soul of the coalition against Napoleon in 1813–14, and who, in 1815, showed himself to be a remarkably effective representative for England at the Treaty of Paris. There's general agreement that the forty years of peace across Europe succeeding Napoleon's downfall are in large part due to Castlereagh's skills as a negotiator.

But as the above verses make plain, Shelley loathed him. And Byron held him in contempt:

> Posterity will ne'er survey
> A nobler grave than this:
> Here lie the bones of Castlereagh:
> Stop, traveller, and ----

Shelley was in Italy when news of what became known as the Peterloo Massacre reached him early in September, 1819, some three weeks after the actual event. There have been any number of detailed accounts as to what happened on August 16th, at St. Peter's Field, on the outskirts of Manchester, but the bare bones are these. Some 60,000 men, women and children turned up for a day of peaceful advocacy for parliamentary reform. They had been summoned to a meeting by Henry ("Orator") Hunt. The meeting, widely advertised in local newspapers and by means of posters and word-of-mouth, was, in Hunt's publicised words, to support "the propriety of adopting the most *legal and effectual* means of obtaining Reform of the Commons House of Parliament." Hunt (1773–1835) was a radical whose constant demands for repeal of the Corn Laws and reform of parliament won him a wide following among the disenfranchised, especially in the industrialising towns and cities of the north. Hence, the 60,000 who, from a fifty-mile radius, turned up at St Peter's Field to hear him speak. As Richard Holmes remarks in his exhaustive *Shelley: The Pursuit*, "many came in organized bands, marching in orderly groups, behind banners and flags, and led by 'radical drill-sergeants' whose experience had been gained during the Napoleonic wars." The banners bore such mottoes as "Liberty and Fraternity", "Parliaments Annual. Suffrage Universal", "Unity and Strength", "Equal Representation or Death", but as all commentators agree, the people were totally unarmed and they came with peaceful intent.

The government, however, wasn't prepared to tolerate what it saw as a dangerously subversive mass meeting. Holmes notes that, at the government's behest, the local magistracy assembled six troops of the 15th Hussars, several companies of the 88th, the whole of the 31st (Infantry) and one troop of Horse Artillery, enough, you feel, to take on a sizeable army. They were there not so much to keep order as to support, if necessary, the local Yeomanry, whom the Home Secretary, Lord Sidmouth, had charged with the responsibility of dispersing the crowds and arresting Hunt. Hunt was, indeed, arrested and subsequently gaoled for two and a half years for "arousing hatred and contempt of the government and the constitution," a judgement much approved by the Liverpool Administration and the Prince Regent, that well-known upholder of law and order.

But the arrest of Hunt turned the day into one of bloody chaos. As the Yeomanry rode up to drag him from his rostrum (he went peacefully), one of the horses knocked down a woman, trampled on her, and killed her child. Not surprisingly the crowd surged in protest around the Yeomanry, at which the mounted Hussars charged in, and by the time they quit the field eleven of the crowd lay dead – sabred, most of them – many hundreds were injured, and still more were badly hurt. According to official reports, there were over 400 such injuries, most of them serious, including those inflicted on at least 100 women and children. Historians agree that the unofficial number of injuries and of deaths resulting from injuries must have been far higher. The Few, armed, mounted, and, in the case of the Yeomanry, out-of-control, servants of the crown, had beaten down the Many. Even *The Times*, which as the historian David Horspool notes in his study *The English Rebel: One Thousand Years of Troublemaking, from the Normans to the Nineties*, was no friend of Hunt, protested that "nearly a hundred [sic] of the King's unarmed subjects have been sabred by a body of cavalry in the streets of a town of which most of them were inhabitants, and in the presence of those Magistrates whose sworn duty it is to protect and preserve the life of the meanest Englishman."

Shelley may well have had those particular words in mind when he sat down to write *The Mask of Anarchy*. According to Holmes, he received a set of English newspapers on September 5th, and almost certainly *The Times*, which like the *Manchester Observer* and *The Examiner* were "especially full in their coverage" of the massacre, would have been among the papers sent to him. Having read the various reports of the events of August 16th, he almost immediately began his poem, and in twelve days had written and clean-copied its ninety-one stanzas. From adolescence he had been a radical (and atheist, which led to his being expelled from Oxford

# THE MASK OF ANARCHY

in 1811) and the events at St Peter's Field spurred him into a period of impassioned creativity during which he wrote not merely the *Mask* but "Peter Bell the Third", his angry satire on, among other things, the apostasy of Wordsworth, as well as his greatest poem, "Ode to the West Wind," that magnificent, troubled prophecy of storm and, eventually, new peace. If winter comes can spring be far behind?

Well, can it? *The Mask of Anarchy* begins with Shelley woken by the sound of "a voice from over the sea,/and with great power it forth led me/To walk in the visions of poesy." The voice is both that of poetry and also the tumultuous voice of the people. And the poem ends with Shelley imagining the voice as erupting, "A volcano heard afar…

> Like Oppression's thundered doom
> Ringing through each heart and brain,
> Heard again—again—again—
>
> "Rise like Lions after slumber
> In unvanquishable number—
> Shake your chains to earth like dew
> Which in sleep had fallen on you—
> Ye are many—they are few."

It is wonderful, stirring stuff, no doubt about it, the rough-hewn ballad measure – so often used in folk and protest ballads of the period – exactly suited to Shelley's hortatory message to and for the people.

Not surprisingly, therefore, the poem, which Shelley sent at once to his radical publisher and friend Leigh Hunt in London, couldn't be published. Hunt, who had already been imprisoned for some scathing remarks about Georgie-Porgie, the Prince Regent, knew that each and every printed copy of the *Mask* would inevitably be seized and that he himself would once again be thrown into gaol. Like so much of Shelley's major work, therefore, *The Mask of*

*Anarchy* never appeared during the poet's lifetime. (It was eventually published in 1832, the year of the Great Reform Act, ten years after the poet's death.) Even Shelley's most radical friends and sympathisers were fearful of helping into print a work that, given the then state of censorship, was certain to cause trouble for its printers, and anyway booksellers wouldn't have dared put the work on sale. Shelley's name was poison to officialdom. When the egregious Robert Southey, that friend of Wordsworth and Coleridge in their early radical days, became Poet Laureate, he took on himself the responsibility of denouncing Shelley and Byron, both of them living in exile in Italy, as "The Satanic School of Poetry." A bad mistake, you feel, given what Byron did to Southey in his "Vision of Judgement," one of the funniest as well as greatest acts of demolition ever visited by one poet on another.

Shelley scorned Southey, but he positively hated Castlereagh. Why? Why *did* he so detest him? True, in the *Mask* Shelley names other members of Liverpool's ministry he judged – rightly – as involved in and at least indirectly responsible for the Peterloo massacre. They include Eldon, Lord Chancellor, and Sidmouth, who, to repeat, as Home Secretary had ordered the meeting to be broken up and Hunt arrested. And yet Castlereagh heads the troupe. It is he who wears the mask of Murder. For Byron, too, Castlereagh is a murderer. Two years after Peterloo, Castlereagh killed himself by cutting his throat with a penknife. I can't remember where I came across the story that it was the Duke of Wellington, by then Prime Minister, who caused Castlereagh's death, by telling him "I feel bound to inform you that you are out of your mind," to which Castlereagh apparently replied "If you say so, it must be so," and promptly put an end to himself.

But even if Byron had heard this story, it wasn't about to make him feel any sympathy for Castlereagh, though he may have permitted himself a moment of admiration for the Iron Duke, whom for the most part he treated with the kind of genial contempt best exemplified in the opening stanzas of Canto Nine of *Don Juan*.

Hearing of Castlereagh's death, Byron produced a series of epigrammatic verses, the best of which is quoted near the start of this Introduction. He also wrote the following:

> So Castlereagh has cut his throat!—The worst
> Of this is,—that his own was not the first.

And

> So *He* has cut his throat at last!—He! Who?
> The man who cut his country's long ago.

To explain this vituperation takes us back to *The Mask of Anarchy*.

In putting Castlereagh at the head of those who oppose the People and use the bloodiest means – murder – to oppress and humiliate them, Shelley is drawing on popular hatred of the man widely known as "the executioner in enamel." Castlereagh had been the cold-blooded represser of the 1798 Irish Rebellion, he was the persecutor of Queen Caroline, who was as much favoured by the many as her errant husband, "Prinny", was scorned by them. He was also at least part-author of "The Six Acts", whose passing into law in June, 1819, gave the government of the day the right to close down any popular meetings or demonstrations to which it took a dislike, which in effect meant most of them. It could also, of course, throw into gaol those found guilty of involvement in, or responsible for, such meetings. The killings and arrests at Peterloo could therefore be regarded as Castlereagh's Acts in operation. No wonder, then, that he was so widely hated, no wonder that when in 1821 his coffin was carried to Westminster Abbey the London crowd cheered it derisively on its way. Shelley's Castlereagh is a metaphor for all that the poet abominated about political oppression.

Hence, the mask. Commentators on the poem have regularly misread its title as indicating that it is on the side of anarchy. It isn't. It's possible, though unlikely, that Shelley was intending an ironic reference to seventeenth-century Masque as a form of high art associated with the Caroline Court, whose avowed intent was to present a masquerade which would endorse the God-given rights of absolute monarchism, even as the country was showing distinct signs of wanting to be rid of Charles. But Shelley certainly wanted to present Castlereagh as the instigator of Anarchy for the very good reason that the high Tory's absolutist tendencies – by which I mean his contempt for democracy – were themselves anarchic in that they dismissed the rights of the people and adapted the law to fit Castlereagh's own concerns. In his great *Dictionary of the English Language* (1755), Samuel Johnson had defined anarchy as "Want of Government; a state in which every man is unaccountable." This is a perfect definition of Castlereagh's indifference to accountability before the bar of wise justice, the justice that operates with the needs and interests of the many in mind. And in *The Mask of Anarchy* Shelley fashioned one of the great, popular poems to champion the many against the few.

There is an irony in this. Shelley is probably the least read of the great Romantic poets. But there can't be many who don't know the closing lines of *The Mask of Anarchy*, even if they don't know who wrote them.

*John Lucas*

# The Mask of Anarchy
## Written on the Occasion of the Massacre at Manchester

As I lay asleep in Italy
There came a voice from over the Sea,
And with great power it forth led me
To walk in the visions of Poesy.

I met Murder on the way—
He had a mask like Castlereagh—
Very smooth he looked, yet grim;
Seven blood-hounds followed him:

All were fat; and well they might
Be in admirable plight,
For one by one, and two by two,
He tossed them human hearts to chew
Which from his wide cloak he drew.

Next came Fraud, and he had on,
Like Eldon, an ermined gown;
His big tears, for he wept well,
Turned to mill-stones as they fell.

And the little children, who
Round his feet played to and fro,
Thinking every tear a gem,
Had their brains knocked out by them.

Clothed with the Bible, as with light,
And the shadows of the night,
Like Sidmouth, next, Hypocrisy
On a crocodile rode by.

And many more Destructions played
In this ghastly masquerade,
All disguised, even to the eyes,
Like Bishops, lawyers, peers, or spies.

Last came Anarchy: he rode
On a white horse, splashed with blood;
He was pale even to the lips,
Like Death in the Apocalypse.

And he wore a kingly crown;
And in his grasp a sceptre shone;
On his brow this mark I saw—
'I AM GOD, AND KING, AND LAW!'

With a pace stately and fast,
Over English land he passed,
Trampling to a mire of blood
The adoring multitude.

And a mighty troop around,
With their trampling shook the ground,
Waving each a bloody sword,
For the service of their Lord.

And with glorious triumph, they
Rode through England proud and gay,
Drunk as with intoxication
Of the wine of desolation.

O'er fields and towns, from sea to sea,
Passed the Pageant swift and free,
Tearing up, and trampling down;
Till they came to London town.

And each dweller, panic-stricken,
Felt his heart with terror sicken
Hearing the tempestuous cry
Of the triumph of Anarchy.

For with pomp to meet him came,
Clothed in arms like blood and flame,
The hired murderers, who did sing
'Thou art God, and Law, and King.

We have waited, weak and lone
For thy coming, Mighty One!
Our purses are empty, our swords are cold,
Give us glory, and blood, and gold.'

Lawyers and priests, a motley crowd,
To the earth their pale brows bowed;
Like a bad prayer not over loud,
Whispering—'Thou art Law and God.'—

Then all cried with one accord,
'Thou art King, and God, and Lord;
Anarchy, to thee we bow,
Be thy name made holy now!'

And Anarchy, the Skeleton,
Bowed and grinned to every one,
As well as if his education
Had cost ten millions to the nation.

For he knew the Palaces
Of our Kings were rightly his;
His the sceptre, crown, and globe,
And the gold-inwoven robe.

So he sent his slaves before
To seize upon the Bank and Tower,
And was proceeding with intent
To meet his pensioned Parliament

When one fled past, a maniac maid,
And her name was Hope, she said:
But she looked more like Despair,
And she cried out in the air:

'My father Time is weak and gray
With waiting for a better day;
See how idiot-like he stands,
Fumbling with his palsied hands!

'He has had child after child,
And the dust of death is piled
Over every one but me—
Misery, oh, Misery!'

Then she lay down in the street,
Right before the horses' feet,
Expecting, with a patient eye,
Murder, Fraud, and Anarchy.

When between her and her foes
A mist, a light, an image rose,
Small at first, and weak, and frail
Like the vapour of a vale:

Till as clouds grow on the blast,
Like tower-crowned giants striding fast,
And glare with lightnings as they fly,
And speak in thunder to the sky,

It grew—a Shape arrayed in mail
Brighter than the viper's scale,
And upborne on wings whose grain
Was as the light of sunny rain.

On its helm, seen far away,
A planet, like the Morning's, lay;
And those plumes its light rained through
Like a shower of crimson dew.

With step as soft as wind it passed
O'er the heads of men—so fast
That they knew the presence there,
And looked,—but all was empty air.

As flowers beneath May's footstep waken,
As stars from Night's loose hair are shaken,
As waves arise when loud winds call,
Thoughts sprung where'er that step did fall.

And the prostrate multitude
Looked—and ankle-deep in blood,
Hope, that maiden most serene,
Was walking with a quiet mien:

And Anarchy, the ghastly birth,
Lay dead earth upon the earth;
The Horse of Death tameless as wind
Fled, and with his hoofs did grind
To dust the murderers thronged behind.

## The Mask of Anarchy

A rushing light of clouds and splendour,
A sense awakening and yet tender
Was heard and felt—and at its close
These words of joy and fear arose

As if their own indignant Earth
Which gave the sons of England birth
Had felt their blood upon her brow,
And shuddering with a mother's throe

Had turnèd every drop of blood
By which her face had been bedewed
To an accent unwithstood,—
As if her heart had cried aloud:

'Men of England, heirs of Glory,
Heroes of unwritten story,
Nurslings of one mighty Mother,
Hopes of her, and one another;

'Rise like Lions after slumber
In unvanquishable number,
Shake your chains to earth like dew
Which in sleep had fallen on you—
Ye are many—they are few.

'What is Freedom?—ye can tell
That which slavery is, too well—
For its very name has grown
To an echo of your own.

"Tis to work and have such pay
As just keeps life from day to day
In your limbs, as in a cell
For the tyrants' use to dwell,

'So that ye for them are made
Loom, and plough, and sword, and spade,
With or without your own will bent
To their defence and nourishment.

"Tis to see your children weak
With their mothers pine and peak,
When the winter winds are bleak,—
They are dying whilst I speak.

"Tis to hunger for such diet
As the rich man in his riot
Casts to the fat dogs that lie
Surfeiting beneath his eye;

"Tis to let the Ghost of Gold
Take from Toil a thousandfold
More than e'er its substance could
In the tyrannies of old.

'Paper coin—that forgery
Of the title-deeds, which ye
Hold to something of the worth
Of the inheritance of Earth.

"Tis to be a slave in soul
And to hold no strong control
Over your own wills, but be
All that others make of ye.

'And at length when ye complain
With a murmur weak and vain
'Tis to see the Tyrant's crew
Ride over your wives and you—
Blood is on the grass like dew.

'Then it is to feel revenge
Fiercely thirsting to exchange
Blood for blood—and wrong for wrong—
Do not thus when ye are strong.

'Birds find rest, in narrow nest
When weary of their wingèd quest;
Beasts find fare, in woody lair
When storm and snow are in the air,[1]

'Asses, swine, have litter spread
And with fitting food are fed;
All things have a home but one—
Thou, Oh, Englishman, hast none!

'This is Slavery—savage men,
Or wild beasts within a den
Would endure not as ye do—
But such ills they never knew.

'What art thou Freedom? O! could slaves
Answer from their living graves
This demand—tyrants would flee
Like a dream's dim imagery:

'Thou art not, as impostors say,
A shadow soon to pass away,
A superstition, and a name
Echoing from the cave of Fame.

'For the labourer thou art bread,
And a comely table spread
From his daily labour come
In a neat and happy home.

'Thou art clothes, and fire, and food
For the trampled multitude—
No—in countries that are free
Such starvation cannot be
As in England now we see.

'To the rich thou art a check,
When his foot is on the neck
Of his victim, thou dost make
That he treads upon a snake.

'Thou art Justice—ne'er for gold
May thy righteous laws be sold
As laws are in England—thou
Shield'st alike the high and low.

'Thou art Wisdom—Freemen never
Dream that God will damn for ever
All who think those things untrue
Of which Priests make such ado.

'Thou art Peace—never by thee
Would blood and treasure wasted be
As tyrants wasted them, when all
Leagued to quench thy flame in Gaul.

'What if English toil and blood
Was poured forth, even as a flood?
It availed, Oh, Liberty,
To dim, but not extinguish thee.

'Thou art Love—the rich have kissed
Thy feet, and like him following Christ,
Give their substance to the free
And through the rough world follow thee,

'Or turn their wealth to arms, and make
War for thy belovèd sake
On wealth, and war, and fraud—whence they
Drew the power which is their prey.

'Science, Poetry, and Thought
Are thy lamps; they make the lot
Of the dwellers in a cot
So serene, they curse it not.

'Spirit, Patience, Gentleness,
All that can adorn and bless
Art thou—let deeds, not words, express
Thine exceeding loveliness.

'Let a great Assembly be
Of the fearless and the free
On some spot of English ground
Where the plains stretch wide around.

'Let the blue sky overhead,
The green earth on which ye tread,
All that must eternal be
Witness the solemnity.

'From the corners uttermost
Of the bonds of English coast;
From every hut, village, and town
Where those who live and suffer moan
For others' misery or their own.[2]

'From the workhouse and the prison
Where pale as corpses newly risen,
Women, children, young and old
Groan for pain, and weep for cold—

'From the haunts of daily life
Where is waged the daily strife
With common wants and common cares
Which sows the human heart with tares—

'Lastly from the palaces
Where the murmur of distress
Echoes, like the distant sound
Of a wind alive around

'Those prison halls of wealth and fashion,
Where some few feel such compassion
For those who groan, and toil, and wail
As must make their brethren pale—

## The Mask of Anarchy

'Ye who suffer woes untold,
Or to feel, or to behold
Your lost country bought and sold
With a price of blood and gold—

'Let a vast assembly be,
And with great solemnity
Declare with measured words that ye
Are, as God has made ye, free—

'Be your strong and simple words
Keen to wound as sharpened swords,
And wide as targes let them be,
With their shade to cover ye.

'Let the tyrants pour around
With a quick and startling sound,
Like the loosening of a sea,
Troops of armed emblazonry.

'Let the charged artillery drive
Till the dead air seems alive
With the clash of clanging wheels,
And the tramp of horses' heels.

'Let the fixèd bayonet
Gleam with sharp desire to wet
Its bright point in English blood
Looking keen as one for food.

'Let the horsemen's scimitars
Wheel and flash, like sphereless stars
Thirsting to eclipse their burning
In a sea of death and mourning.

'Stand ye calm and resolute,
Like a forest close and mute,
With folded arms and looks which are
Weapons of unvanquished war,

'And let Panic, who outspeeds
The career of armèd steeds
Pass, a disregarded shade
Through your phalanx undismayed.

'Let the laws of your own land,
Good or ill, between ye stand
Hand to hand, and foot to foot,
Arbiters of the dispute,

'The old laws of England—they
Whose reverend heads with age are gray,
Children of a wiser day;
And whose solemn voice must be
Thine own echo—Liberty!

'On those who first should violate
Such sacred heralds in their state
Rest the blood that must ensue,
And it will not rest on you.

'And if then the tyrants dare
Let them ride among you there,
Slash, and stab, and maim, and hew,—
What they like, that let them do.

## The Mask of Anarchy

'With folded arms and steady eyes,
And little fear, and less surprise,
Look upon them as they slay
Till their rage has died away.

'Then they will return with shame
To the place from which they came,
And the blood thus shed will speak
In hot blushes on their cheek.

'Every woman in the land
Will point at them as they stand—
They will hardly dare to greet
Their acquaintance in the street.

'And the bold, true warriors
Who have hugged Danger in wars
Will turn to those who would be free,
Ashamed of such base company.

'And that slaughter to the Nation
Shall steam up like inspiration,
Eloquent, oracular;
A volcano heard afar.

'And these words shall then become
Like Oppression's thundered doom
Ringing through each heart and brain,
Heard again—again—again—

'Rise like Lions after slumber
In unvanquishable number—
Shake your chains to earth like dew
Which in sleep had fallen on you—
Ye are many—they are few.'

## Notes

1 (p20) This additional stanza is found here in the Wise manuscript – a not-quite-complete draft in Shelley's handwriting – and in Mary Shelley's edition of 1839.

> 'Horses, oxen, have a home,
> When from daily toil they come;
> Household dogs, when the wind roars,
> Find a home within warm doors.'

2 (p23) This additional stanza is found (cancelled) here in the Wise manuscript.

> 'From the cities where from caves,
> Like the dead from putrid graves,
> Troops of starvelings gliding come,
> Living Tenants of a tomb.'